2011 Breeding Season Report for Pinnacles National Monument – Prairie Falcons and Other Raptors

Natural Resource Technical Report NPS/SFAN/NRTR—2012/614

Gavin Emmons

National Park Service
Pinnacles National Monument
5000 Highway 146
Paicines, California 95043

August 2012

U.S. Department of the Interior
National Park Service
Natural Resource Stewardship and Science
Fort Collins, Colorado

The National Park Service, Natural Resource Stewardship and Science office in Fort Collins, Colorado publishes a range of reports that address natural resource topics of interest and applicability to a broad audience in the National Park Service and others in natural resource management, including scientists, conservation and environmental constituencies, and the public.

The Natural Resource Technical Report Series is used to disseminate results of scientific studies in the physical, biological, and social sciences for both the advancement of science and the achievement of the National Park Service mission. The series provides contributors with a forum for displaying comprehensive data that are often deleted from journals because of page limitations.

All manuscripts in the series receive the appropriate level of peer review to ensure that the information is scientifically credible, technically accurate, appropriately written for the intended audience, and designed and published in a professional manner. This report received informal peer review by subject-matter experts who were not directly involved in the collection, analysis, or reporting of the data. Data in this report were collected and analyzed using methods based on established, peer-reviewed protocols and were analyzed and interpreted within the guidelines of the protocols.

Views, statements, findings, conclusions, recommendations, and data in this report do not necessarily reflect views and policies of the National Park Service, U.S. Department of the Interior. Mention of trade names or commercial products does not constitute endorsement or recommendation for use by the U.S. Government.

This report is also available from the San Francisco Bay Area Network (http://www.nature.nps.gov/im/units/SFAN) and the Natural Resource Publications Management website (http://www.nature.nps.gov/publications/NRPM) on the Internet.

Please cite this publication as:

Emmons, G. 2012. 2011 Breeding season report for Pinnacles National Monument – prairie falcons and other raptors. Natural Resource Technical Report NPS/SFAN/NRTR—2012/614. National Park Service, Fort Collins, Colorado.

NPS 114/116504, August 2012

Contents

Contents (continued)

Figures

Tables

Appendices

Executive Summary

Pinnacles National Monument ("Pinnacles") provides a diverse habitat for numerous cliff-nesting raptors, including prairie falcons (*Falco mexicanus*), peregrine falcons (*F. peregrinus*) and golden eagles (*Aquila chrysaetos*), as well as a spectacular array of summits and cliff-wall routes for rock-climbers. This monitoring effort was established to determine long-term trends in the number of occupied territories and productivity of nesting prairie falcons. Ancillary data on presence and diversity of other nesting raptors are also collected. The effort grew out of a need to reduce potential disturbance that climbers and off-trail hikers may have on cliff-nesting raptors. This report summarizes the results from the 2011 breeding season and represents the 26th year of monitoring at the monument, consistent with the standardized methods and procedures detailed in the Prairie Falcon Monitoring Protocol for Pinnacles National Monument (Emmons et al. 2011).

To monitor falcons, field technicians surveyed all potential nest sites three times per breeding season spaced 21-28 days apart. Nests determined to be active were revisited to confirm rearing of nestlings and fledging of young. In 2011, monitoring was conducted from 1 January 2011 until 13 July 2011, with a total of over 150 possible and active nest sites monitored during 808 observation hours.

Prairie falcon occupancy and nesting productivity in 2011 were consistent with and slightly above average compared to the results documented for the previous 25 years of implementing the Pinnacles raptor monitoring program. Thirteen territorial falcon pairs were documented this year with 12 pairs actively nesting. Eight nests successfully hatched and fledged 33 young; 4 nests failed.

For other raptor species nesting in the monument, 33 breeding pairs representing 10 raptor species were observed in the 2011 season in addition to prairie falcons. A peregrine falcon pair nested and hatched 3 young in the Hawkins territory, but the nest failed prior to fledging of young.

Two golden eagle pairs were observed occupying historical territories at Pinnacles in 2011, and 1 successful nest attempt at North Chalone Peak produced 2 nestlings with fledge of at least 1 young likely. Nests for additional sensitive California species were recorded this season for Cooper's hawks (*Accipiter cooperii*), sharp-shinned hawks (*A. striatus*), white-tailed kites (*Elanus leucurus*), and long-eared owls (*Asio otus*). Other nesting raptor species documented in the monument included red-tailed hawks (*Buteo jamaicensis*), red-shouldered hawks (*B. lineatus*), American kestrels (*F. sparverius*), great-horned owls (*Bubo virginianus*), and barn owls (*Tyto alba*).

Acknowledgements

This program would not be as successful as it is without the eyes and ears of helpful Pinnacles employees. Therefore, I would like to thank the NPS employees for their help, encouragement, and passion for the raptors and wildlife diversity at Pinnacles. The many local climbers involved with Friends of Pinnacles also deserve my thanks for their ongoing support of resource protection and breeding raptors at the park and particularly their efforts to publicize and honor advisories in effect. I would also like to extend my appreciation to the monument visitors, for their reports and observations on raptor sightings and for their appreciation and value of the importance of monitoring, managing, and protecting the nesting sites and breeding productivity of raptors in the monument.

I would like to thank Alacia Welch, Daniel George, Dan Ryan, Jess Auer, Scott Scherbinski, Jennie Jones, Paul Johnson, Brent Johnson, Linda Regan, Jenn Tiehm, and Sarah Reid for contributing valuable observations on raptor territories and pair behavior in the monument. I greatly appreciated efforts by Tessa Christensen and Ronnie Johnson to advertise and secure volunteers for the raptor monitoring program, and Kristen Swehla for her volunteer efforts this season. I am also grateful for Denise Louie's and Paul Johnson's support and efforts, in tandem with Marcus Koenen as the manager of the Inventory and Monitoring (I&M) Program, to keep the Pinnacles raptor monitoring program funded annually and on a permanent basis. As the interim I&M manager after Marcus' departure, Jeff Runde's and Marie Denn's efforts in continuing to honor and support the raptor monitoring efforts at Pinnacles were also greatly appreciated. Penny Latham, Steve Fancy, and Paul Johnson also provided recommendations and reviewer suggestions for the 2011 annual report, contributing greatly to a concise and efficient document consistent with I&M standards.

The following staff also shared their experience, excitement, and observations of raptors with me throughout the season, granting me a more complete picture of raptor breeding and diversity at the monument, and assisted in the effective management of raptor advisory areas: Roberto Cruz, Giasonne Gigliotti, Mark Lashelle, Debbie Simmons, Joseph Smith, and Eric Falquist.

Introduction

Pinnacles National Monument ("Pinnacles") is a National Park Service unit located in the Gabilan Mountains of central California, and provides a diverse habitat for cliff-nesting raptor species, including sensitive species such as prairie falcons, peregrine falcons, and golden eagles. The dramatic landscapes, extensive trails, arrays of summits, and cliff-wall routes at Pinnacles are also used intensively for recreation by rock-climbers and hikers.

Many scientific studies have documented the negative impacts of human disturbance of raptor nest and roost sites, and the resulting nest failures and territorial abandonment associated with these disturbances. Nesting raptor species at Pinnacles sensitive to human disturbance include prairie falcons (Fyfe and Olendorff 1976, Ogden and Hornocker 1977, Harmata et al. 1978, Sitter 1983, Steenhof 1998), peregrine falcons (particularly in remote locations: see Hickey 1942, 1969, Bond 1946, Steenhof 1998), golden eagles (Newton 1979, 1990, Scott 1985, Steidl et al. 1993, Watson 1997, Steenhof et al. 1997, Kochert et al. 1999), sharp-shinned hawks (Delannoy and Cruz 1988), and long-eared owls (Marks 1986, Marti and Marks 1989, Bloom 1994).

Studies of prairie falcon nest occupancy and productivity have also shown the species to be especially sensitive to human disturbance from mining (Becker and Ball 1981, Bednarz 1984), recreation (Boyce 1982), agriculture (USDI 1979), habitat destruction and nest site limitation (Becker and Ball 1981, Steenhof et al. 1997), and proximity to major roadways (Platt 1974, Boyce 1982).

The main sources of human disturbance of nesting raptors at Pinnacles are visitors that are rock-climbing and hiking on- and off-trail in the monument. Scientific studies have consistently suggested that these recreation activities can be balanced against raptor nesting by establishing closure or advisory areas that act as buffers between human activity and raptor nesting during the breeding season (Fyfe et al. 1976, Olsen and Olsen 1978, Becker and Ball 1981, Suter and Joness 1981, Porter et al. 1987, Holthuijzen et al. 1990, Cade et al. 1996, White et al. 2002). Raptor monitoring program survey data collected at Pinnacles justifies the establishment of climbing/hiking advisories in core areas (high visitor-use areas) each breeding season as a way to protect cliff-nesting raptor species from human disturbance.

The Prairie Falcon Monitoring Protocol for Pinnacles National Monument (Emmons et al. 2011) was formally peer-reviewed and approved in 2010, with final revisions completed in 2011. This protocol provides standardized methods and procedures for prairie falcon monitoring at Pinnacles and further details the program specifics. An introduction to the program objectives is briefly described below.

Monitoring efforts began initially to establish annual climbing/hiking advisories in core areas. The program established two long-term monitoring objectives to:

- Track changes in the total numbers of territorial prairie falcon pairs in core areas and non-core areas.

- Track changes in average annual productivity (young of year hatched/pair, young of year at banding age/pair, young of year fledged/pair) in core areas and non-core areas.

Core areas are locations at Pinnacles suitable for prairie falcon cliff-nesting where climbing impacts could occur, based on the presence of historic climbing routes accessible to visitors. Non-core areas refer to all other areas within Pinnacles suitable for cliff-nesting. The core vs. non-core sampling design is detailed further in the Methods section.

A secondary benefit of the monitoring program is that a substantial amount of information can also be gathered on other raptor species at Pinnacles, particularly sensitive California species that may be impacted by human presence and disturbance in riparian habitats such as: Cooper's hawks, sharp-shinned hawks, white-tailed kites, and long-eared owls. Breeding data for other raptor species is documented according to the Prairie Falcon Monitoring Protocol for Pinnacles National Monument (Emmons et al. 2011) with incidental observations during falcon surveys and a small investment of additional time for area searches during foot travel between falcon activity sites. Additional monitoring of breeding efforts by other raptor species is covered by Pinnacles base-funding and includes observations by the raptor technician, interns, volunteers, and other Pinnacles employees. Although lack of consistent nesting data for these species over the course of the 26-year raptor monitoring program precludes statistical and trend analysis, the presence data nevertheless provide valuable information on the diversity and location of breeding raptors at Pinnacles. This has been used for planning purposes relating to the revision of the General Management Plan (GMP), and for guiding timing of routine maintenance activities.

Study Area and Field Methods

Pinnacles is located in the Gabilan Mountains of the central Coast Range of California. The national monument encompasses 10,694 hectares (26,425 acres) with elevation ranging from 244 to 1007 meters (800 to 3304 feet). The climate is Mediterranean with hot, dry summers and cool, damp winters. Temperatures range from a mean of 5.2°C in December to 25.2°C in August (41.4° to 77.4°F). The average yearly rainfall is 44 cm (17.4 inches), with the majority of rainfall occurring from November to April (NOAA 2000).

Pinnacles provides a diverse range of habitat types for birds and other species. These habitats include: volcanic rock formations and outcroppings, California mixed chaparral, pine-oak woodlands, grasslands, and riparian habitats.

Sample Design

The prairie falcon monitoring focuses on core areas and non-core areas. Core areas (Figure 1) are locations in Pinnacles that can support prairie falcon cliff-nesting, and where impacts to raptors due to rock climbing activities can occur based on historic rock-climbing use and access. Core area sampling is conducted through a census, because the area is sufficiently small to allow for complete coverage.

Non-core areas refer to all other areas within the monument that can support prairie falcon cliff-nesting. The Prairie Falcon Monitoring Protocol for Pinnacles National Monument (Emmons et al. 2011) calls for sampling non-core territories on a rotating basis. For 2003-2011, non-core area sampling has been conducted through a census along with core area sampling. This has been possible because of comprehensive historical data on prairie falcon nest sites gathered over the past 26 years, extensive monitoring experience of the raptor technician, and supplemental raptor monitoring efforts by interns, volunteers, and other Pinnacles employees covered by Pinnacles base-funding. In addition, GIS modeling completed in 2008 confirmed that all potential prairie falcon nesting areas in the monument have been surveyed annually during the past 8 years.

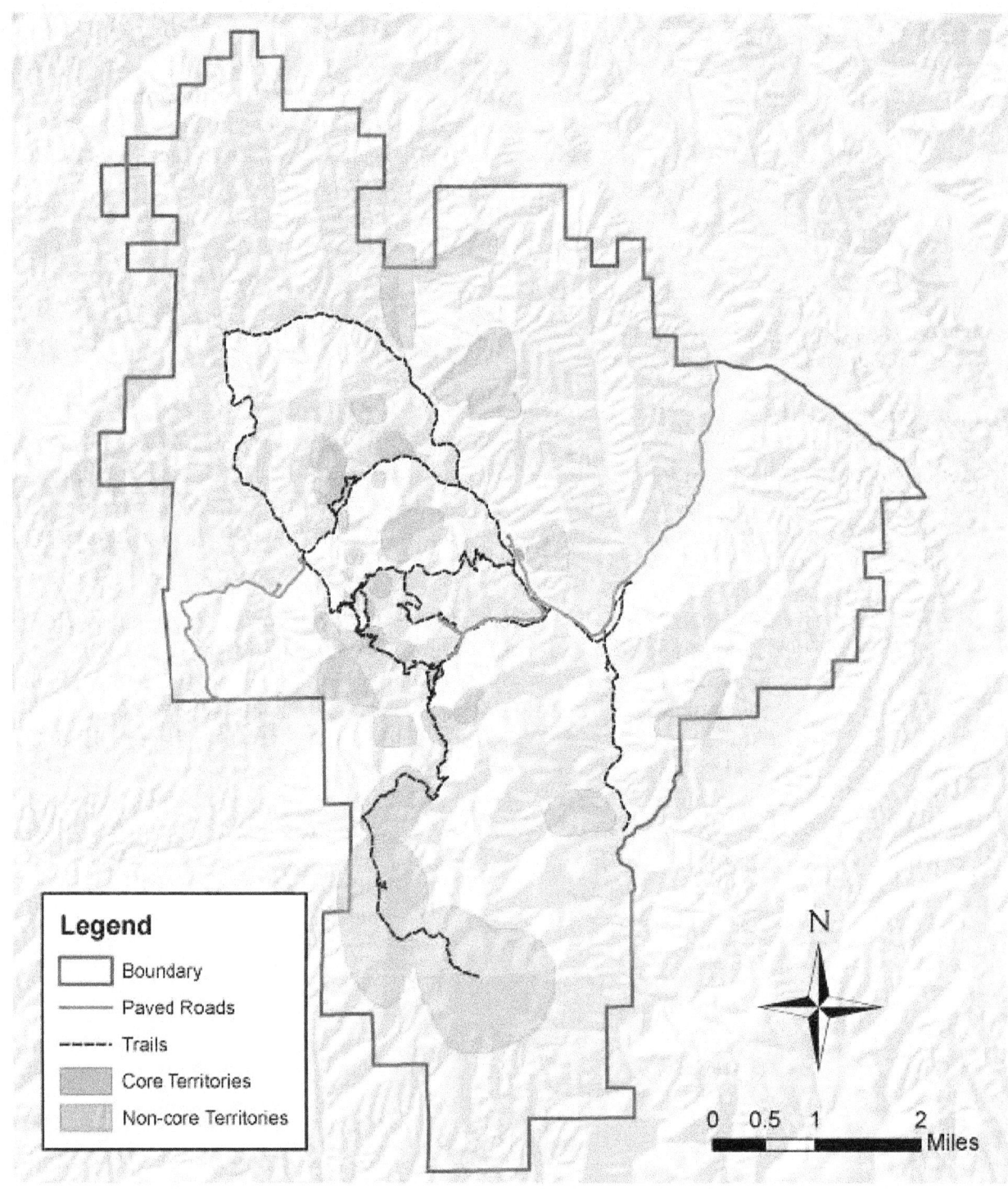

Figure 1. Core and non-core areas at Pinnacles National Monument.

Field Methods

Survey methods followed the standard operating procedures detailed in the Prairie Falcon Monitoring Protocol for Pinnacles National Monument (Emmons et al. 2011).

Prairie Falcons

Potential and established prairie falcon territories in core and non-core areas were surveyed using Swarovski STS-60 HD 20-60x spotting scopes and Zeiss Victory FL 10x42 binoculars. Observations were made from the locations that provided the best view of an eyrie or a territory. A Magellan Triton 500 GPS unit was used to plot every observation point. Field data were documented with standardized datasheets and field notebooks and the data were entered into a standardized database (Appendix D).

Three- to five-hour observation periods are commonly recommended to document territorial occupancy of peregrine falcons and prairie falcons (USFWS 1984, Cade et al. 1996, Smith et al. 2006). Steenhof et al. (1999) employed 2-hour observation periods during point surveys to document territory occupancy of prairie falcons in the Snake River region of Idaho. For a potential prairie falcon territory to be classified as unoccupied at Pinnacles, we adopted a conservative standard of visiting potential nest sites at least 3 times per breeding season spaced 21-28 days apart to confirm territorial occupancy, courtship, and incubation of eggs within a breeding season (Fuller and Mosher 1981, Fraser et al. 1983, Steenhof 1998). Survey duration was ultimately dependent upon visibility but at least three 4-hour surveys (12 hours total) were required to verify that "no birds" were present. Nests determined to be active were revisited to confirm rearing of nestlings and fledging of young. Nests in core areas were monitored more frequently and during weekend days when climbers were more likely to be present.
While other monitoring programs infer fledging success at 90% fledge age (Steenhof and Kochert 1982, Anderson and Squires 1997, Steenhof 1998), our protocol continues surveys until all young falcons are confirmed as fledged.

During the prairie falcon breeding season status was asserted as follows:

Territories: Territorial behavior included perching, flying, territorial disputes and defense, stooping and scold calling, and roosting locations.

Courtship: Courtship behavior included copulation, food drops and swapping, and potential nest site inspections and preparation.

Incubation: Incubation status was determined by observing prairie falcons flying into a nest hole and not re-emerging for extended periods of time. During this time, egg counts were made whenever possible (e.g., when lighting conditions allowed and when incubating falcons temporarily left the nest during food drops and/or nest switches). Soft incubation – the onset of incubation – was determined by a small number of eggs laid and the female incubating for short durations (15-75 minutes of incubation and 20 minutes or more not incubating the eggs). Hard incubation was characterized by the adult falcons – primarily the females – incubating a full clutch of eggs for hours in duration.

Nestlings: Hatched young prairie falcons were aged by physical features using an aging guide (Moritsch 1983). Hatch dates were determined by counting backwards from at least 2 (preferably 3 or more) independent agings.

Fledging: Fledging was confirmed by seeing young perched and/or in flight away from the nest site. Fledging dates were estimated by the coordination and strength of flight, the size of perches, and the amount of vocalization during flight.

Other Raptors

All data for raptor species other than prairie falcons were collected on an ancillary basis. Riparian- and cliff-nesting activity for all species other than prairie falcons was documented en route to observation points for prairie falcon monitoring, and supplemented by base-funded monitoring conducted by the raptor technician, interns, volunteers, and other Pinnacles employees. Additionally, Pinnacles staff/visitor observations of breeding raptor activity were checked for confirmation of raptor presence.

Potential and established raptor territories were surveyed using spotting scopes (20-60x) and binoculars (10x42). Observations were made from locations where breeding raptor activity was documented and raptor nest sites were most visible. A Magellan Triton 500 GPS unit was used to plot observation points.

For all raptor species other than prairie falcons, potential nesting habitat was visited at least two times per breeding season spaced 21-28 days apart. Visits were scheduled to correspond with general phenology patterns for egg incubation and nesting per species to allow for the highest possibility of confirming territorial occupancy and active nesting of raptor species. Active nest sites were revisited approximately every 28 days to document rearing of nestlings and fledging of young.

Monitoring Schedule

The prairie falcon monitoring season started on 1 January and continued through the end of the nesting season, 13 July (Table 1).

Table 1. Timing of nesting behavior of prairie falcons at Pinnacles National Monument.

Behavior	January	February	March	April	May	June	July
Territorial Falcons							
Courtship Behavior							
Nesting							
Fledging							

Weather was always an important factor. During temperature extremes, heavy fog, or rain, most birds of prey were not active and therefore monitoring was not done during these periods.

Data Management

Data are entered into a Microsoft (MS) Access database designed by the Network Data Manager for the San Francisco Bay Area Network Inventory and Monitoring Program. Original data sheets are archived with Pinnacles Resource Management. An annual (static) copy of the Access database is archived on the Golden Gate National Recreation Area computer network drive. Nest data are also submitted to the California Department of Fish and Game (CDFG) California National Diversity Database, and the Santa Cruz Predatory Bird Research Group.

Tabular data in the Results section of this report are derived from queries to the Breeding Raptors and Raptor Observations tables in the MS Access database.

Climbing Advisories

Climbing advisories went into effect by mid-January. Informational signs were established near territories occupied by prairie falcons at least once during the preceding 3 years. Visitors were advised to avoid these areas but compliance was voluntary. Advisory areas with posted signs (Figure 2) included the Balconies, Hawkins, Scout Peak, Frog/Hand, Discovery Wall, and Little Pinnacles territories.

Figure 2. Setting up advisory sign. Photo by Gavin Emmons, 2006.

Results

Prairie Falcons

During the 2011 field season, Pinnacles staff spent 480 hours in the field surveying for prairie falcons and volunteers contributed 54 hours of time. The number of prairie falcon nests and productivity this year were consistent with and slightly higher than the 26-year running average rates. Twelve prairie falcon pairs attempted to nest this year and 8 successful nests produced 33 nestlings and fledglings, compared to 26-year averages of 9.9 nesting pairs, 7.8 successful nests, 28.5 nestlings, and 26.7 fledglings (Table 2).

Occupied Territories

Through the 2011 season 13 territorial pairs of prairie falcons (Figure 3) were confirmed over the course of the breeding season. This number is comparable to the average territorial occupancy of 11.9 territories from 1984-2011 (Table 2). Of these, one pair did not nest or produce young this year. A single pair occupied the Frog/Hand and Discovery Wall territories but abandoned both by April.

Core Areas: In 2011 there were 8 territorial prairie falcon pairs within the core areas. This number is similar to the number of territorial falcon pairs (7.4) in the core areas over the last 26 years.

Non-Core Areas: In 2011 there were 5 territorial prairie falcon pairs within the non-core areas. This number is similar to the number of territorial falcon pairs (4.5) in the non-core areas over the last 26 years.

Figure 3. Prairie falcon fledgling at South Balconies. Photo by Gavin Emmons, 2009.

Table 2. 1984-2011 Pinnacles prairie falcon nesting productivity – core and non-core areas combined.

Year	Territorial Pairs	Nesting Pairs	Successful Nests	# Nestlings	# Nestlings / Nest	# Fledglings	# Fledglings / Nest
1984	10	9	8	30	3.8	27	3.4
1987	6	4	4	13	3.3	10	2.5
1988	12	9	8	24	3	24	3
1989	12	12	9	24	2.7	21	2.3
1990	14	10	8	31	3.9	29	3.6
1991	14	11	10	34	3.4	34	3.4
1992	13	11	10	38	3.8	34	3.4
1993	13	12	10	39	3.9	35	3.5
1994	13	13	12	45	3.8	42	3.5
1995	13	11	8	24	3	24	3
1996	12	10	9	35	3. 9	34	3.8
1997	12	8	6	26	4.3	26	4.3
1998	10	7	0	0	0	0	0
1999	10	8	6	25	4.2	25	4.2
2000	8	8	7	22	3.1	22	3.1
2001	10	10	7	24	3.4	24	3.4
2002	11	9	7	26	3.7	22	3.1
2003	12	9	8	33	4.1	32	4
2004	12	11	9	36	4	33	3.7
2005	13	10	9	29	3.2	24	2.7
2006	15	14	10	35	3.5	30	3
2007	14	12	9	35	3.9	33	3.7
2008	12	5	4	12	3	12	3
2009	12	11	10	41	4.1	37	3.7
2010	13	11	7	27	3.9	27	3.9
2011	13	12	8	36	4.5	33	4.1
Averages (1984-2011)	11.9	9.9	7.8	28.6	3.5	26.7	3.3

Annual Productivity

Twelve of the 13 prairie falcon pairs nested. Of the 12 nesting pairs, eight had successful nesting attempts and fledged a total of 33 nestlings (Tables 2, 3). The number of fledglings was slightly higher than the 26-year average of 26.7 fledglings (Figure 4). Four nests failed during the 2011 season, three during egg incubation and one after 3 total nestlings hatched.

Table 3. 2011 Pinnacles prairie falcon breeding summary.

Territory	Nest Used/ Last Year Used	# Eggs Laid	# Young Hatched	# Young Known/ Fledged
Drywall	DRY-11/2010	4	4	4/ 4
Crowley Towers*	CT-1/ 2010	4	4	4/ 4
Pig Canyon	PIG-1/ 1998		0	0
Little Pinnacles*	LP-8/ 2010		0	0
Canyon North of Willow Springs	CNWS-3/ 2010	5	5	5/ 5
South Balconies*	SGB-2/ 2006	4	4	4/ 4
Resurrection Wall*	RW-1/ 2006	4	4	4/ 4
General Balconies*	SGB-17/ NEW	3	3	3/ 3
Citadel*	CI-1/ 2006	4	4	4/ 4
Tunnel*	TU-1/ 1994	3	3	0
South Chalone	SC-7/ 2010		0	0
North Chalone	NC-1/ 2010	5	5	5/ 5

*nests within the core area.

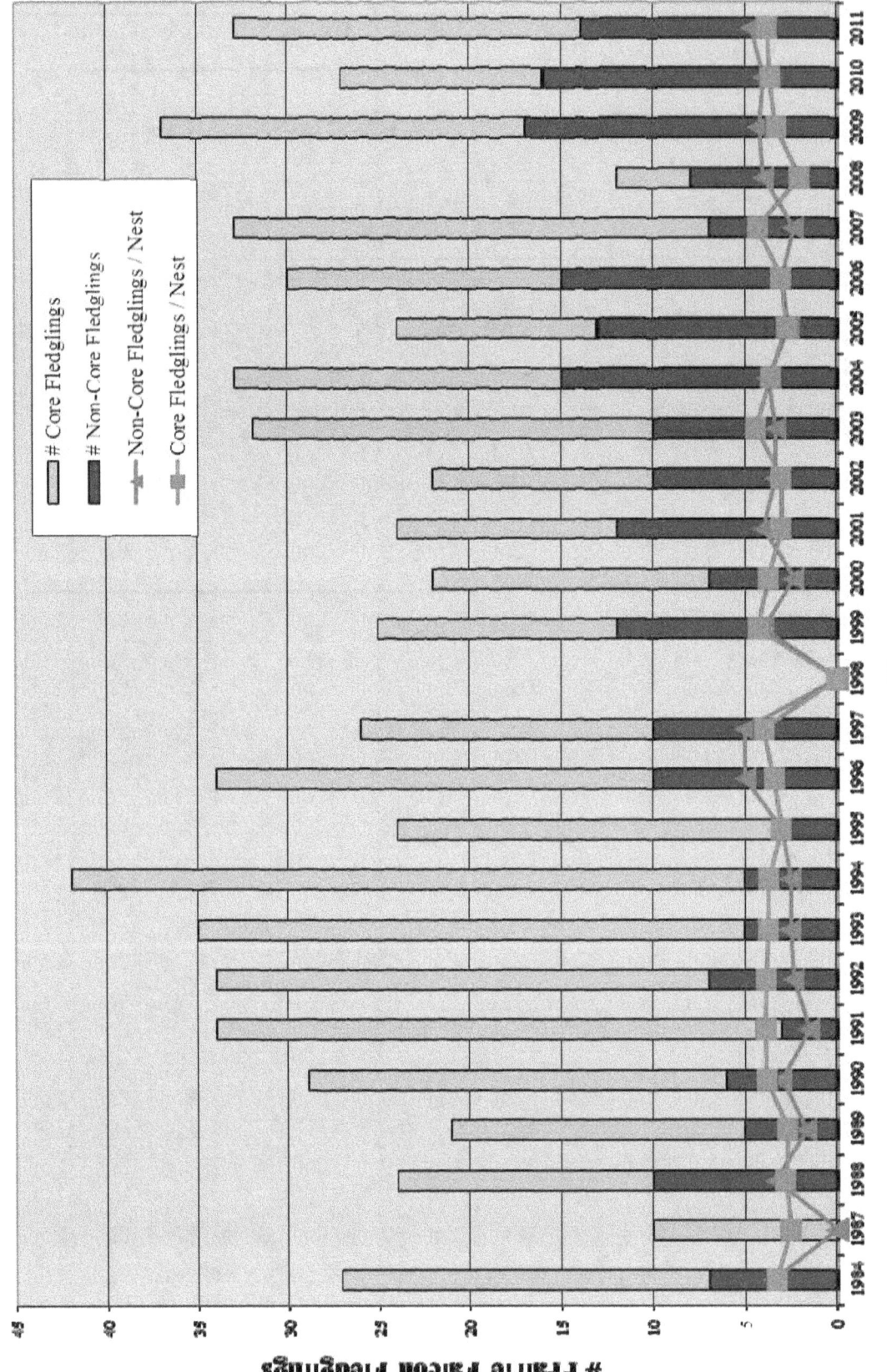

Figure 4. Core vs. non-core Pinnacles PRFA fledgling productivity, 1984-2011.

Nesting falcon pairs, total successful nests, and productivity of nestlings and fledglings within core areas this season were consistent with the 26-year averages. Additionally, nestlings and fledglings per nest were slightly above average. In the core areas only, five successful nest sites produced 19 total fledglings and 3.8 fledglings per nest, compared to the 26-year averages of 5.2 successful nests, 18.0 total fledglings, and 3.3 fledglings per nest (Table 4).

Core Areas: Of the 8 territorial falcon pairs in the core areas in 2011, five nested successfully, producing an average of 3.8 fledglings per nest (Table 4). Productivity numbers are consistent with the 1984-2011 averages of 5.2 successful nests per season and slightly higher than the averages of 3.3 fledglings per nest.

Non-Core Areas: Of the 5 territorial falcon pairs in the non-core areas in 2010, three nested successfully, producing an average of 4.7 fledglings per nest (Table 5). These numbers are higher than the 1984-2011 averages of 2.7 successful nests per season and 3.3 fledglings per nest.

Table 4. 1984-2011 Pinnacles prairie falcon nesting productivity – core areas only.

Year	Territorial Pairs	Nesting Pairs	Successful Nests	# Nestlings	# Nestlings / Nest	# Fledglings	# Fledglings / Nest
1984	7	6	6	22	3.7	20	3.3
1987	5	4	4	13	3.3	10	2.5
1988	8	6	5	14	2.8	14	2.8
1989	8	8	6	16	2.7	16	2.7
1990	9	7	6	23	3.8	23	3.8
1991	9	8	8	31	3.9	31	3.9
1992	9	7	7	29	4.1	27	3.9
1993	10	9	8	34	4.3	30	3.8
1994	10	10	10	38	3.8	37	3.7
1995	10	9	7	21	3	21	3
1996	9	8	7	28	4	24	3.4
1997	8	6	4	16	4	16	4
1998	7	5	0	0	0	0	0
1999	6	5	3	13	4.3	13	4.3
2000	5	5	4	15	3.8	15	3.8
2001	7	6	4	12	3	12	3
2002	5	5	4	12	3	12	3
2003	5	5	5	22	4.4	22	4.4
2004	7	7	5	21	4.2	18	3.6
2005	6	5	4	12	3	11	2.8
2006	7	6	5	17	3.4	15	3
2007	6	6	6	26	4.3	26	4.3
2008	7	3	2	4	2	4	2
2009	7	7	6	24	4	20	3.3
2010	8	6	3	11	3.7	11	3.7
2011	8	7	5	19	3.8	19	3.8
Averages (1984-2011)	7.4	6.4	5.2	19.0	3.5	18.0	3.3

Table 5. 1984-2011 Pinnacles prairie falcon nesting productivity – non-core areas only.

Year	Territorial Pairs	Nesting Pairs	Successful Nests	# Nestlings	# Nestlings / Nest	# Fledglings	# Fledglings / Nest
1984	3	3	2	8	4	7	3.5
1987	1	0	0	0	0	0	0
1988	4	3	3	10	3.3	10	3.3
1989	4	4	3	8	2.7	5	1.7
1990	5	3	2	8	4	6	3
1991	5	3	2	3	1.5	3	1.5
1992	4	4	3	9	3	7	2.3
1993	3	3	2	5	2.5	5	2.5
1994	3	3	2	7	3.5	5	2.5
1995	3	2	1	3	3	3	3
1996	3	2	2	7	3.5	10	5
1997	4	2	2	10	5	10	5
1998	3	2	0	0	0	0	0
1999	4	3	3	12	4	12	4
2000	3	3	3	7	2.3	7	2.3
2001	3	4	3	12	4	12	4
2002	6	4	3	14	4.7	10	3.3
2003	7	4	3	11	3.7	10	3.3
2004	5	4	4	15	3.8	15	3.8
2005	7	5	5	17	3.4	13	2.6
2006	8	8	5	18	3.6	15	3
2007	8	6	3	9	3	7	2.3
2008	5	2	2	8	4	8	4
2009	5	4	4	17	4.3	17	4.3
2010	5	5	4	16	4	16	4
2011	5	5	3	14	4.7	14	4.7
Averages (1984-2011)	4.4	3.5	2.7	9.5	3.3	8.7	3.0

Phenology
The first prairie falcon pairs were observed at Goat Rock and Teapot Dome on 1 January 2011 (Appendix A). Incubation was first observed at South Balconies on 22 March. The first hatching occurred between 13-15 April at the General Balconies and South Balconies nests. The first fledging took place from 25-27 May at General Balconies and South Balconies. The last fledging took place at Citadel on 18-20 June when 4 young fledged from a late season nesting effort.

Other Notes
Eleven of the 12 eyries chosen by prairie falcons were used in previous years. All prairie falcon eyries were within historically documented territories. Four nesting attempts failed this year, likely due to predation. Four territories occupied by prairie falcon pairs in the past 5 years – Pipsqueak Pinnacles, Narrows, Marion Canyon, and Mating Rocks – were vacant this year.

Other Raptors
During the 2011 field season, Pinnacles staff spent 174 hours in the field surveying for other raptors and volunteers contributed 100 hours of time. Observers documented 12 territorial raptor species at Pinnacles in addition to prairie falcons. Of these, 10 species were documented as

breeding at Pinnacles (Table 6) including 6 species of concern tracked by the California Natural Diversity Database (CDFG 2011). Ten breeding raptor species and 33 nest sites were documented at Pinnacles in 2011. For all breeding raptor species other than prairie falcons, twelve previously undocumented nest sites were confirmed. Although level of effort for other raptor species varies from year to year and results have not been standardized against effort levels, more breeding pairs and species were observed this year than in most previous years.

Throughout the prairie falcon breeding season, ancillary data were collected on other raptor species nesting at Pinnacles. Notes are presented below. See Appendices B and C for further phenology and breeding data.

Table 6. 2011 Pinnacles nesting productivity for species other than prairie falcons.

Species	Territorial Pairs	Nesting Pairs	Successful Nests	# Fledglings	# Fledglings / Nest
Peregrine Falcon *	1	1	0	N/A	N/A
Golden Eagle *	2	1	1	1	1.0
Red-tailed Hawk	11	10	8	23	2.9
American Kestrel	17	4	2	7	3.5
Red-shouldered Hawk	6	5	3	7	2.3
Cooper's Hawk *	4	3	2	4	2.0
Sharp-shinned Hawk *	1	1	1	4	4.0
White-tailed Kite *	4	2	2	4	2.0
Western Screech-Owl	3	Unknown	Unknown	N/A	N/A
Barn Owl	3	1	Unknown	N/A	N/A
Great-horned Owl	5	3	3	6	2.0
Long-eared Owl *	2	1	1	4	4.0

* Species of Concern tracked by California Natural Diversity Database.

Peregrine Falcon
A peregrine falcon (Figure 5) pair occupied and successfully nested in the Hawkins territory, marking the 7th consecutive year that a peregrine pair nested in the monument. The pair was first observed courting, perching, and circling near Hawkins Peak on 1 January 2011. The pair was previously observed September through December 2010, suggesting the falcons were resident at the monument through the winter season. Through mid-March, the peregrine falcon pair copulated often, inspected historical nest sites at Hawkins regularly, and actively stooped other raptors in the Hawkins territory. The peregrine falcon pair hatched 3 young by late April but the

nest failed in late May, likely due to predation. Prior to the last 7 years, a previously confirmed peregrine falcon nest effort at Pinnacles was documented in 1957.

Figure 5. Juvenile peregrine falcon. Photo by Gavin Emmons, 2005.

Golden Eagle

Golden eagle pairs were observed occupying historical territories on the west side of North Chalone Peak and at the Eucalyptus Grove outside of the west entrance of Pinnacles. The golden eagle pair at North Chalone Peak successfully hatched 2 young by early May. Fledging of the young eaglets was not confirmed but highly likely given observations of the young near fledging age. Golden eagle adults and juveniles were active throughout the monument. Historical nest sites in three territories – Frog Canyon, South Chalone Peak, and Eagle Rock – containing five former nest sites were surveyed in mid-winter through late spring, with no new greenery added to any of the nests.

Red-tailed Hawk

Twelve red-tailed hawk pairs (Figure 6) were observed occupying territories at Pinnacles in 2011. Ten nesting pairs were confirmed and 8 pairs successfully produced 23 fledglings. Historical nest sites at the Western Front, Guard Rock, and West Side Entrance were not occupied or used this year. A red-tailed hawk pair occupied the High Peaks West Of Chalone territory this year but did not nest in the area. All 10 active red-tailed hawk nests were made of sticks and located at Eagle Rock, Hand, Kingman Land North, McCabe Canyon, North Balconies, North Wilderness Trail, South Wilderness North, South Wilderness Rock, and Upper Condor Gulch. Nest sites at Kingman Land North and South Wilderness Rock were previously undocumented. The other eight nests had been used by red-tailed hawk pairs in previous years. The red-tailed hawk pairs at Eagle Rock and Upper Condor Gulch began egg incubation but failed to hatch any young.

Figure 6. Juvenile red-tailed hawk. Photo by Gavin Emmons, 2005.

American Kestrel

Seventeen territorial pairs and 4 active nests were confirmed for American kestrels this year. Nesting pairs were observed at Discovery Wall, Mating Rocks, Neglected Valley, and South Wilderness Trail. The Discovery Wall and Neglected Valley nests were documented at historical sites. The other 2 nests were previously undocumented. The Mating Rocks site hatched young on 3-5 May, and the Discovery Wall site hatched young on 13-17 May. Hatching dates were not otherwise confirmed. Ten nestlings were confirmed at 4 nests: five at Discovery Wall, four at the Mating Rocks nest, two at the South Wilderness Trail nest, and 1 young at the Neglected Valley nest. At least 1 fledgling from the Discovery Wall nest and all fledglings from the Mating Rocks nest were confirmed. Other kestrel pairs for which nesting was not confirmed occupied the following territories: D. Soto Canyon, Drywall, Eucalyptus Grove, High Peaks West Of Chalone, Kingman Land North, Marion Canyon, North Chalone, Pig Canyon, Resurrection Wall, Scout Peak, South Balconies, Teapot Dome, and Upper Condor Gulch.

Red-shouldered Hawk

Six territorial red-shouldered hawk pairs were documented in the monument this year at the following territories: Bench Area, Kingman Land South, McCabe Canyon, Pinnacles Campground, Regan Ranch Canyon, and South Wilderness Trail. The McCabe Canyon, Pinnacles Campground, and Regan Ranch Canyon nests were previously undocumented. All nests were built along riparian corridors in pine/oak woodland habitat. The first territorial red-shouldered hawk pairs were observed at the Bench Area on 25 February 2011. No nesting was confirmed for the red-shouldered hawk pair occupying the South Wilderness Trail territory this year. The other 5 red-shouldered hawk pairs nested this year, with 3 nests successfully producing fledglings. Seven Nestlings were confirmed at the 3 successful red-shouldered hawk nests, with full fledge confirmed at every nest. The Kingman Land South red-shouldered hawk pair nested successfully at the north end of the Pinnacles Campground, and a second hawk pair nested at the south end of the campground. This latter red-shouldered hawk pair and the Regan Ranch Canyon red-shouldered hawk pair began egg incubation but failed due to nest abandonment.

Cooper's Hawk

Four territorial pairs and 3 active nests were confirmed for Cooper's hawks (Figure 7) at Pinnacles in 2011. Cooper's hawk pairs occupied the following territories: Kingman Land North,

Kingman Land South, Marion Canyon, and South Wilderness Trail. The stick nests were built along riparian corridors in the Kingman Land North, Marion Canyon, and South Wilderness Trail territories. The Marion Canyon nest was last used in 2010, and the other 2 nests were previously undocumented. The Kingman Land North and Marion Canyon Cooper's hawk nests hatched 4 nestlings, with full fledge confirmed from both nests. The nesting Cooper's hawk pair at the South Wilderness Trail territory incubated eggs but failed to hatch any young, likely due to nest abandonment. Nesting was not confirmed for the Cooper's hawk pair occupying the Kingman Land South territory. Historical territories at North Wilderness Trail, Grassy Canyon, and Upper Bear Gulch were not occupied this year.

Figure 7. Cooper's hawk nestling in Marion Canyon nest. Photo by Gavin Emmons, 2008.

Sharp-shinned Hawk

One sharp-shinned hawk (Figure 8) nest was confirmed at Pinnacles in 2011. The nesting pair was first observed defending the Peaks View Area territory and incubating eggs on 13 May 2010. Four nestlings were observed at the previously undocumented nest site, and full fledging was confirmed on 6 July. The stick nest was located in a pine/live oak grove near sharp-shinned hawk nest sites used in the past 3 years.

Figure 8. Juvenile sharp-shinned hawk. Photo by Gavin Emmons, 2003.

White-tailed Kite

Four territorial pairs and 2 active nests were confirmed for white-tailed kites at Pinnacles in 2011. White-tailed kite pairs occupied the Jawbone Canyon, Kingman Land South, McCabe Canyon, and South Wilderness (North End) territories. Stick nests built on live oaks near open grassland ad riparian habitat were confirmed at the Jawbone Canyon and Kingman Land North territories. The Jawbone Canyon nest was previously used in 2006, and the Kingman Land North nest was previously undocumented. The white-tailed kite nests hatched 4 young, and full fledging was confirmed at both nests. White-tailed kite pairs occupied the McCabe Canyon and South Wilderness (North End) territories, but no active nesting was confirmed. Three historical white-tailed kite territories were not occupied in 2011: Double Gates, Kingman Land North, and Marion Canyon. The white-tailed kite nests confirmed in 2011 were the first documented for the species at Pinnacles since 2007.

Long-eared Owl

Three pairs of long-eared owls (Figure 9) were documented this year at the following territories: Grassy Canyon, Kingman Land North, and McCabe Canyon. One active stick nest built on a live oak in riparian habitat was confirmed at the Kingman Land North territory. Four owl nestlings hatched on 1-5 April and full fledge was confirmed on 23 April. No active nests were confirmed for the long-eared owl pairs occupying the Grassy Canyon and McCabe Canyon territories. Historical nest sites at Marion Canyon were not occupied in 2011.

Figure 9. Long-eared owl adult near Chalone housing area. Photo by Gavin Emmons, 2006.

Barn Owl

A nesting barn owl pair was documented at a historical site at D. Soto Canyon in 2011. Egg incubation was observed on 22 February, but hatching of nestlings was not confirmed. Barn owl pairs occupied the Grassy Canyon and Kingman Land South territories, but nest sites were not confirmed. Historical sites at Drywall, Discovery Wall, and the High Peaks Trail West of Chalone Housing were unoccupied.

Figure 10. Barn owl nestlings near fledging. Photo by Gavin Emmons, 2006.

Great-horned Owl

Great horned owls were documented vocalizing and occupying territories at Chalone Picnic Area, High Peaks Trail West of Chalone Housing, Guard Rock, Kingman Land North, McCabe Canyon, and North Wilderness Rock in 2011. Nesting was confirmed at High Peaks Trail West of Chalone Housing, McCabe Canyon, and North Wilderness Rock. The High Peaks Trail West of Chalone Housing nest was a historically documented site, and the other two nest sites were previously undocumented for great-horned owls. The McCabe Canyon nest was a stick nest on a live oak in riparian habitat (used by red-shouldered hawks in 2010), and the other two owl nests were cliff-cavity sites. The 3 nests produced a total of 6 nestlings, with full fledge confirmed at the McCabe Canyon and North Wilderness Rock nests. Full fledge at the High Peaks Trail West of Chalone Housing nest was likely but not confirmed. Historical territories at Machete Ridge, South Balconies, South Wilderness (South End), and Upper Condor Gulch were unoccupied.

Figure 11. Great-horned owl nestling. Photo by Gavin Emmons, 2009.

Western Screech Owl (Megascops kennicottii)
Screech owls were seen and heard hooting at the Chalone Housing Area, Upper Bear Gulch, and near the Bear Gulch Nature Center beginning in January. No breeding or nest records were confirmed for 2011.

Northern Harrier (Circus cyaneus)
A northern harrier female was observed soaring and circling low in upper Grassy Canyon in early January.

Northern Pygmy-Owl (Glaucidium gnoma)
A northern pygmy-owl was heard hooting in the riparian habitat near the Sandy Creek crossing of the fire road throughout the spring, but no pair status or breeding activity was confirmed.

Discussion

Combined prairie falcon occupancy and productivity in core and non-core areas this year were generally consistent with the 26-year running average rates. Twelve prairie falcon pairs attempted to nest this year and eight successful nests produced 33 nestlings and fledglings, compared to 26-year averages of 9.9 nesting pairs, 7.8 successful nests, 28.5 nestlings, and 26.7 fledglings (Table 2).

In core areas, numbers for successful nests, nestlings, and fledglings were average in 2011 (Table 4). In non-core areas, respective numbers were above average in 2011 (Table 5). Total productivity numbers in the core and non-core areas were affected by 4 nest failures, with 2 each at core area nest sites. One core area nest site failed during development of nestlings, and the two non-core area nest sites failed during egg incubation. All 3 of these nest sites were in close geographic proximity to each other (and to the single peregrine falcon nest that failed after producing nestlings). Given the inaccessible locations of the nest sites, the lack of any human activity observed at the sites through the breeding season, and the proximity of the nest sites, the nest failures were likely due to predation (e.g., from eagles, ravens, or owls), especially given the documentation of territorial and nesting great-horned owls in the area. However, given the lack of constant monitoring at the sites (e.g., through remote video surveillance), nest failure due to human disturbance cannot be entirely ruled out.

The second core area nest failure occurred during egg incubation, but was confirmed when a common raven was observed scavenging the remains of the adult female prairie falcon at the nest site. This nest failure was likely due to predation, given the inaccessible nature of the cliff-cavity nest and the nature of the nest failure. Although rodenticide poisoning—through ingestion of poisoned prey—could have contributed to the nest failure, no direct observations were available and insufficient tissue material was collected at the site after the nest failure to confirm this.

For raptors other than prairie falcons, ten breeding raptor species and 33 nest sites were documented at Pinnacles in 2011. Although these numbers are higher than averages recorded in the past 8 years, all data gathered for other raptor species were ancillary and are therefore difficult to interpret conclusively.

Conclusions, Management Implications and Recommendations

Climbing management actions, outreach, and recommendations for further management and research are listed below. Refer to Appendix E for further information on public interest highlights for the 2011 season.

Prairie Falcons: Climbing Advisories

Climbing advisories were put in place in January in areas with historic climber usage to protect nesting raptors from disturbance. In March and April advisories were updated and lifted in territories that were confirmed unoccupied by prairie and peregrine falcon pairs. Signs detailing climbing advisories were posted at Little Pinnacles, Balconies, Hawkins, Discovery Wall, Scout Peak, Frog/Hand, Crowley Towers, Egg, Tunnel, Teapot Dome, Pipsqueak Pinnacles, and Goat Rock/Resurrection Wall territories.

Due to the large size and climber popularity of Machete Ridge, a partial advisory was instituted at this territory. A partial advisory was also instituted at Balconies after two nest sites were confirmed at South and General Balconies respectively. Machete Ridge and the North Balconies were opened to climber use after the Balconies falcon pairs had shifted to focus territorial and nesting efforts at the South and General Balconies nest sites.

All regular advisory signs were affixed to metal brackets and cement foundations to prevent theft, and none were vandalized in 2011.

In 2011, two incidents of off-trail hikers in advisory areas were documented. Two incidents involving climbers were also documented, at Machete Ridge and South Balconies. The climbers involved were contacted by law enforcement rangers and retreated from the areas after having climbing advisory policies clarified. No territorial defense behavior by prairie falcons was observed.

Human / Falcon Interactions and Nest Failures

Prairie and peregrine falcon adults in the North Chalone Peak, Crowley, Hawkins, and Balconies territories responded to the presence of on-trail hikers and raptor biologists with agitated behavior by circling and wailing above their respective territories.

Prairie falcon nest entries were conducted at the North Chalone Peak and South Balconies nests by the NPS Raptor Biologist and raptor researcher Douglas Bell from East Bay Regional Park District (see Public Interest Highlights below for further details). All nestlings at these 2 eyries fledged successfully. All falcon nestlings at the Crowley and General Balconies nests also fledged successfully.

Four prairie falcon nest failures were documented at the Tunnel, Little Pinnacles, Pig Canyon, and South Chalone Peak territories. Tunnel nest failed when the nestlings at the sites were 2-3 weeks old, and the other 3 nests failed during egg incubation. Causes of the falcon nest failures in 2011 were not confirmed, but could potentially include nest predation (by ravens, eagles, or owls), abandonment, or significant human disturbance. All 4 nests were not accessible by on-trail hikers. The Pig Canyon, Tunnel, and South Chalone Peak nests had no historic climbing routes directly adjacent to the nest sites. The Little Pinnacles nest had rarely used climbing routes next to the eyrie but there were no signs of climber use at or near the site throughout the 2011 season, and the nature of the nest failure – with the scavenged remains of the adult female found at the site – strongly suggested predation rather than human disturbance or abandonment.

Education Opportunities

Throughout the year, the raptor biologist and park staff participated in public outreach opportunities to inform visitors about raptor conservation. Educational opportunities included participation in formal events (e.g., Rockpile Rendezvous on April 22-24) and informal events (e.g., visitor contact in high-use areas such as High Peaks, Balconies Cliff Trail, and the Bear Gulch Reservoir).

Management Recommendations

- Continue to establish climbing/hiking advisories in core areas (high visitor-use areas) each breeding season to protect cliff-nesting raptor species from human disturbance.

- Increase information opportunities for visitor use assistants and park rangers to educate park visitors about advisories. Prior to the 2004 season, the park made more attempts to speak with climbers and hikers at trailheads, and to regularly rove on trails to provide interpretation and enforcement of resources.

- Enforce advisories with law enforcement rangers. Although advisories are voluntary, disturbing wildlife is a citable offense that law enforcement rangers should continue to employ to discourage visitors from willfully threatening nesting efforts of breeding raptors at Pinnacles.

- Increase field staff. While the monitoring program focuses on the status and trends of prairie falcons, the park is interested in additional data on non-target species. In order to monitor non-target species adequately, at least 1 other 0.5 FTE field technician is needed during the breeding season.

- Increase use of staff and visitors to observe raptor activity in the field. This can be achieved through regular communication with NPS staff and visitors, bi-weekly monitoring updates on raptor status at the monument, and reminders about filling out wildlife observation cards.

Recommendations for Future Monitoring and Research

Historically, the raptor monitoring program has focused on managing for the protection of cliff-nesting raptors, particularly prairie falcons and golden eagles, because they are species of concern in California and are directly impacted by climbing advisories in the monument. The standardization of raptor monitoring procedures and raptor advisories, and effective communication with hikers and climbers at the monument, has helped to ensure the continuing breeding success of prairie falcons and golden eagles, and the return of breeding peregrine falcons to the monument. However, four sensitive species of concern in California – Cooper's hawks, sharp-shinned hawks, white-tailed kites, and long-eared owls – have received little monitoring attention historically, despite the confirmation of active nesting for all of these species. These 4 raptor species tend to reproduce along riparian corridors where many of the trails are located and potential disturbance of nest sites by visitors should be studied further. Fletcher (2003) conducted graduate-level fieldwork on accipiter nest site selection and recreational trail use at Pinnacles in 1999-2001. He documented 20 nests and two nest failures along trails in the monument, and recommended further studies to determine the effects of visitor disturbance on accipiter breeding in the monument.

As the staff at Pinnacles continue to transition into managing the bottomlands extending out to Highway 25, the need for further monitoring of forest and woodland nesting raptors becomes even more important. Much of this new monument property contains riparian corridors and oak/pine woodlands suitable for accipiter, kite, and long-eared owl nesting habitat. Recommendations for monitoring of riparian-nesting raptor species include:

- Inventory nest sites for species of concern in riparian habitats in the monument.

- Determine what percentage of riparian raptor nests occur along trails and in high-use visitor areas relative to low-use areas, and how breeding behavior and productivity rates compare in high- and low-use areas.

- Recommend that new trails, buildings, and visitor use areas avoid documented nest sites and likely nesting habitat for riparian raptor species, based on results from inventory and research data above.

Without this baseline information, it may be necessary for resource managers at Pinnacles to enforce seasonal closures of these new developments in order to protect these species from disturbance.

Other recommendations for monitoring and research:

- Conduct an inventory of burrowing owls on recently acquired Pinnacles Ranch property. This owl is also listed as a sensitive species of concern in many western states including California (Martell 1990, James 1992, Haug et al. 1993), with local populations in California – particularly near the San Francisco Bay and the Central Valley – declining steeply in recent years (Johnson 1992). The first record for burrowing owls in the monument was documented in October 2006 on the western boundary near the Bear Gulch Headwaters. These owls may also inhabit the rangeland and fields between the Pinnacles Campground and Highway 25. Field work could be done by a biological science technician or by extending the raptor biologist through September or October.

- Determine potential threats to prairie falcons nesting at Pinnacles. Radio telemetry studies conducted from 2002-2005 revealed important preliminary data about the prairie falcon population at Pinnacles: the population is resident in or near the monument throughout the year, and all radio-tracked falcons fed primarily on prey items just south and west of the monument boundaries, with no evidence of adult falcons feeding north or east of the monument (Buranek 2006). This information suggests that alteration of habitat south and west of the monument boundaries, especially near the town of Soledad, could have significant negative consequences for a viable, long-term population of prairie falcons at Pinnacles. In addition, the effects of pesticide (e.g., rodenticide) in the area are poorly understood.

Literature Cited

Anderson, S. H., and J. R. Squires. 1997. The prairie falcon. University of Texas Press. Austin, Texas.

Becker, D. M., and I. J. Ball. 1981. Impacts of surface mining on prairie falcons: Recommendations for monitoring and mitigation. Montana Cooperative Wildlife Research Unit Unpublished Report, Montana State University, Missoula.

Bednarz, J. C. 1984. Effect of mining and blasting on breeding prairie falcon (*Falco mexicanus*) occupancy in the Caballo Mountains, New Mexico. Raptor Research 18:16–19.

Bloom, P. H. 1994. The biology and current status of the long-eared owl in coastal southern California. Bulletin California Academy of Science 93:1–12.

Bond, R. M. 1946. The peregrine populations of western North America. Condor 48:101–116.

Boyce, D. A., Jr. 1982. Prairie falcon fledgling productivity in the Mojave Desert, California. Thesis. Humboldt State University, Arcata, California.

Buranek, S. 2006. Pinnacles prairie falcon home range and habitat analysis. Thesis. California State University, Sacramento, California.

Cade, T. J., J. H. Enderson, and J. Linthicum. 1996. Guide to management of peregrine falcons at the eyrie. The Peregrine Fund, Boise, Idaho.

California Department of Fish and Game (CDFG). 2011. Special Animals. Available at http://www.dfg.ca.gov/biogeodata/cnddb/pdfs/SPAnimals.pdf. (accessed 5 October 2011).

Delannoy, C. A., and A. Cruz. 1988. Breeding biology of the Puerto Rican sharp-shinned hawk (*Accipiter striatus venator*). Auk 105:649–662.

Emmons, G., J. Pettersen, M. Koenen, and D. Press. 2011. Prairie falcon monitoring protocol for Pinnacles National Monument: narrative – version 2.3. Natural Resource Report NPS/SFAN/NRR—2011/466. National Park Service, Fort Collins, Colorado.

Fletcher, C. 2003. Accipiter nest site selection and recreational trail use effects at Pinnacles National Monument. Thesis. California Polytechnic State University, San Luis Obispo, California.

Fraser, J. D., L. D. Frenzel, J. E. Mathisen, F. Martin, and M. E. Shough. 1983. Scheduling bald eagle reproduction surveys. Wildlife Society Bulletin 11:13–16.

Fuller, M. R., and J. A. Mosher. 1981. Methods of detecting and counting raptors: a review. Studies in Avian Biology 6:235–246.

Fyfe, R. W., and R. R. Olendorff. 1976. Minimizing the dangers of nesting studies to raptors and other sensitive species. Canadian Wildlife Service Occasional Papers No. 23:1–17.

Harmata, A. R., J. E. Durr, and H. Geduldig. 1978. Home range, activity patterns and habitat use of Prairie Falcons nesting in the Mojave Desert. Colorado Wildlife Services Unpublished Report, Fort Collins, Colorado for U.S. Department of the Interior, Bureau of Land Management, Riverside, California (Contract No. YA-512-CT8-4389).

Haug, E. A., B. A. Millsap, and M. S. Martell. 1993. Burrowing owl (*Athene cunicularia*). The Birds of North America, No. 61. Cornell Laboratory of Ornithology, Ithaca, New York.

Hickey, J. J. 1942. Eastern population of the duck hawk. Auk 59: 176–204.

Hickey, J. J. 1969. Peregrine falcon populations: their biology and decline. University of Wisconsin Press, Madison, Wisconsin.

Holthuijzen, A. M. A., W. G. Eastland, A. R. Ansell, M. N. Kochert, R.D. Williams, and L. S. Young. 1990. Effects of blasting on behavior and productivity of nesting prairie falcons. Wildlife Society Bulletin 18:270–281.

James, P. C. 1992. Operation burrowing owl in Saskatchewan: The first five years. Abstract, Burrowing Owl Symposium. Raptor Research Foundation Annual Meeting, Seattle, Washington, 1992.

Johnson, B. S. 1992. Characterization of population and family genetics of the burrowing owl by DNA fingerprinting. Abstract, Burrowing Owl Symposium. Raptor Research Foundation Ann. Meeting, Seattle, Washington, 1992.

Kochert, M. N., K. Steenhof, L. B. Carpenter, and J. M. Marzluff. 1999. Effects of fire on golden eagle territory occupancy and reproductive success. Journal of Wildlife Management 63:773–780.

Marks, J. S. 1986. Nest-site characteristics and reproductive success of long-eared owls in southwestern Idaho. Wilson Bulletin 98:547–560.

Martell, M. S. 1990. Reintroduction of burrowing owls into Minnesota: A feasibility study. Thesis. University of Minnesota, Minneapolis, Minnesota.

Marti, C. D. and J. S. Marks. 1989. Medium-sized owls. Proceedings of the Western Raptor Management Symposium and Workshop. National Wildlife Federation Science and Technology Series No. 12, Washington, D.C.:124–133.

Moritsch, M. Q. 1983. Photographic guide for aging nesting prairie falcons. United States Department of the Interior, Bureau of Land Management, Snake River Birds of Prey Project. Boise District, Idaho.

National Oceanic and Atmospheric Administration (NOAA). 2000. Pinnacles National Monument station. Climatological Data: California, 1971–2000. National Oceanic and Atmospheric Administration, Washington D.C. Available from http://www.ncdc.noaa.gov/normals.html (accessed 17 September 2010).

Newton, I. 1979. Population ecology of raptors. Buteo Books. Shipman, Virginia.

Newton, I. 1990. Birds of prey. Facts on File, Inc. New York, New York.

Ogden, V. T., and M. G. Hornocker. 1977. Nesting density and success of prairie falcons in southwestern Idaho. Journal of Wildlife Management 41:1–11.

Olsen, P., and J. Olsen. 1978. Alleviating the impact of human disturbance on the breeding peregrine falcon. Ornithologists Corella 2(1):1–7 and 4(3):54–57.

Platt, S. W. 1974. Breeding status and distribution of the prairie falcon in northern New Mexico. Thesis. Oklahoma State University, Stillwater, Oklahoma.

Porter, R. D., M. A. Jenkins, and A. L. Ganski. 1987. Working bibliography of the peregrine falcon. National Wildlife Federation Science and Technology Series No. 9, Washington, D.C.

Scott, T. A. 1985. Human impacts on the golden eagle population of San Diego County. Thesis. San Diego State University, San Diego, California.

Sitter, G. 1983. Feeding activity and behavior of prairie falcons in the Snake River Birds of Prey Natural Area in southwestern Idaho. Thesis. University of Idaho, Moscow, Idaho.

Smith, J. P., and A. Hutchins. 2006. Northeast Nevada Nest Survey 2005. Hawkwatch International, Inc., Salt Lake City, Utah. Available from http://www.hawkwatch.org/publications/Technical%20Reports/NNNS%20Report%202005.pdf (accessed 20 September 2008).

Steenhof, K. 1998. Prairie falcon (*Falco mexicanus*). The Birds of North America, No. 346. Cornell Laboratory of Ornithology, Ithaca, New York.

Steenhof, K., and M. N. Kochert. 1982. An evaluation of methods used to estimate raptor nesting success. Journal of Wildlife Management 46:885–893.

Steenhof, K., M. N. Kochert, L. B. Carpenter, and R. N. Lehman. 1999. Long-term prairie falcon population changes in relation to prey abundance, weather, land uses, and habitat conditions. Condor 101:28–41.

Steenhof, K., M. N. Kochert, and T. L. McDonald. 1997. Interactive effects of prey and weather on golden eagle reproduction. Journal of Animal Ecology 66:350–362.

Steidl, R. J., K. D. Kozie, G. J. Dodge, T. Pehovski, and E. R. Hogan. 1993. Effects of human activity on breeding behavior of golden eagles in Wrangell-St. Elias National Park and Preserve; a preliminary assessment. WRST Research and Resource Management Report No. 93-3. National Park Service, Wrangell-St. Elias National Park and Preserve, Copper Center, Alaska.

Suter, G. W., and J. L. Joness. 1981. Criteria for golden eagle, ferruginous hawk, and prairie falcon nest site protection. Raptor Research 15:12–18.

United States Department of the Interior (USDI). 1979. Snake River Birds of Prey special research report to the Secretary of the Interior. Boise District Bureau of Land Management, Boise, Idaho.

United States Fish and Wildlife Service (USFWS). 1984. American peregrine falcon Rocky Mountain/Southwest population recovery plan. Rocky Mountain/Southwest Peregrine Falcon Recovery Team, U.S. Fish and Wildlife Service, Denver, Colorado.

Watson, J. 1997. The golden eagle. London, United Kingdom.

White, C. M., N. J. Clum, T. J. Cade, and W. G. Hunt. 2002. Peregrine falcon (*Falco peregrinus*). The Birds of North America Online (A. Poole, Ed.). Cornell Laboratory of Ornithology, Ithaca, New York. Available at http://bna.birds.cornell.edu/BNA/account/Peregrine_Falcon (accessed 8 September 2008).

Appendix A. 2011 nest phenology and success for prairie falcons.

Nest Species	Territory Occupied	Nest Code	Arrival Date	Begin Incub	Hatch Date	Fledge Date	Abandon Date	Failed Date	# of Eggs	# of Nestlings	Known Fledglings	Possible Fledglings	Occup. Status
PRFA	Ball Pinnacle												Not Occ.
PRFA	Cyn N of Willow Spgs	CNWS-3	<1/13	<4/2	4/15-17	5/27-29			5	5	5	5	5
PRFA	Central High Peaks												Not Occ.
PRFA	Citadel	CI-1	<3/22	<3/29	5/7-9	6/18-20				4	4	4	4
PRFA	Crowley Drainage												Not Occ.
PRFA	Crowley Towers	CT-1	<1/7	<4/3	4/18-19	5/30-31				4	4	4	4
PRFA	D. Soto Canyon												Not Occ.
PRFA	Deserted Valley												Not Occ.
PRFA	Discovery Wall	*FROG	<1/12										Occupied
PRFA	Drywall	DRY-11	<1/4	<3/25	4/21-23	6/2-4			4	4	4	4	4
PRFA	Egg	*TU-1	<1/1										Occupied
PRFA	Frog Canyon												Not Occ.
PRFA	Frog / Hand	*DIS	<1/12										Not Occ.
PRFA	General Balconies	SGB-17	<1/19	<4/13	4/13-15	5/25-27				3	3	3	3
PRFA	Goat Rock	*RW-1	<1/1										Occupied
PRFA	Guard Rock												Not Occ.
PRFA	Hanging Valley												Not Occ.
PRFA	Hawkins												Not Occ.
PRFA	High Pks W of CPA												Not Occ.
PRFA	Little Pinnacles	LP-8	<1/6	<4/5				5/4-25			0	0	Failed
PRFA	Machete	*SGB-17	<1/19										Occupied
PRFA	Marion Canyon												Not Occ.
PRFA	Mating Rocks												Not Occ.
PRFA	Narrows												Not Occ.
PRFA	NE Sec 15	*NC-1	<1/15										Occupied
PRFA	Neglected Valley												Not Occ.
PRFA	North Balconies												Not Occ.

Appendix A. 2011 nest phenology and success for prairie falcons (continued).

Nest Species	Territory Occupied	Nest Code	Arrival Date	Begin Incub	Hatch Date	Fledge Date	Abandon Date	Failed Date	# of Eggs	# of Nestlings	Known Fledglings	Possible Fledglings	Occup. Status
PRFA	North Chalone	NC-1	<1/15	<3/31	4/15-17	5/27-29				5	5	5	5
PRFA	North Wilderness Rock												Not Occ.
PRFA	Pig Canyon	PIG-1	<2/3	<3/30				<5/16		0	0	0	Failed
PRFA	Pipsqueak Pinnacles												Not Occ.
PRFA	Prescribed Burn Cliffs	*RW-1	<1/1										Occupied
PRFA	Resurrection Wall	RW-1	<1/1	<3/28	4/25-26	6/6-7			4	4	4	4	4
PRFA	Scout Peak	*RW-1	<1/1										Occupied
PRFA	South Balconies	SGB-2	<1/19	<3/22	4/13-15	5/25-27				4	4	4	4
PRFA	South Chalone	SC-7	<3/31	<3/31				<4/29			0	0	Failed
PRFA	S. Wilderness Rock												Not Occ.
PRFA	Teapot Dome	*TU-1	<1/1										Occupied
PRFA	Tugboat												Not Occ.
PRFA	Tunnel	TU-1	<1/1	<3/28	4/14-18			<5/16		3	0	0	Failed
PRFA	Upper Bear Gulch												Not Occ.
PRFA	Upper Condor Gulch												Not Occ.
PRFA	Western Front												Not Occ.
PRFA	Willow Spring Slide	*CNWS-3	<1/13										Occupied

Note: for the "Occup. Status" column, # refers to possible fledglings, "Occupied" = territorial occupation, "Not Occ." = no occupation, "Failed" = failed nest, "Abandon" = territory abandoned after confirmed occupancy, "Unknown" = breeding confirmed (see nest code) or likely, but nest status unknown. For the "Nest Code" column, * refers to territorial links for raptor pairs occupying more than 1 territory

Appendix B. 2011 nest phenology and success for peregrine falcons, American kestrels, golden eagles, and buteos.

Nest Species	Territory Occupied	Nest Code	Arrival Date	Begin Incub	Hatch Date	Fledge Date	Abandon Date	Failed Date	# of Eggs	# of Nestlings	Known Fledglings	Possible Fledglings	Occup. Status
PEFA	Hawkins Peak	HP-2	<1/1	<3/28	4/23-25			<5/31	3	3	0	0	Failed
AMKE	Citadel		<1/19										Occupied
AMKE	D. Soto Canyon		<2/22										Occupied
AMKE	Discovery Wall	DIS-4		<4/18	5/13-17	6/9-13			5	5	1	5	5
AMKE	Drywall		<1/4										Occupied
AMKE	Eucalyptus Grove		<1/19										Occupied
AMKE	High Pks W of CPA		<1/2										Occupied
AMKE	Kingman Land North		<4/9										Occupied
AMKE	Marion Canyon		<3/17										Occupied
AMKE	Mating Rocks	MAT-4	<1/31		5/3-5	5/29-6/1				2	2	2	2
AMKE	Neglected Valley	NV-2	<2/6		<5/30					1	0	0	Unknown
AMKE	North Chalone		<3/7										Occupied
AMKE	Pig Canyon		<3/9										Occupied
AMKE	Resurrection Wall		<1/22										Occupied
AMKE	Scout Peak		<3/4										Occupied
AMKE	South Balconies		<3/1										Occupied
AMKE	South Wilderness Trail	SWT-8	<3/15		<6/2					2	0	0	Unknown
AMKE	Teapot Dome		<3/4										Occupied
AMKE	Upper Condor Gulch		<2/8										Occupied
GOEA	Eucalyptus Grove		<1/19										Occupied
GOEA	North Chalone	NCW-1	<1/21		4/31-5/7	6/12-15				2	0	2	2
RTHA	Eagle Rock	ER-2	<1/13	<4/3				<5/19			0	0	Failed
RTHA	Frog / Hand	HAND-1	<1/15	<4/6	4/14-16	5/30-6/1				3	2	3	3
RTHA	Grassy Canyon	*SWN-2	<1/4										Occupied
RTHA	High Pks W of CPA		<2/1										Occupied
RTHA	Kingman Land North	KLN-4		<3/18	4/3-5	5/18-20				4	3	4	4
RTHA	Kingman Land North	KLN-14		<4/1	4/1-3	5/17-19				2	2	2	2

Appendix B. 2011 nest phenology and success for peregrine falcons, American kestrels, golden eagles, and buteos (continued).

Species	Territory Occupied	Nest Code	Arrival Date	Begin Incub	Hatch Date	Fledge Date	Abandon Date	Failed Date	# of Eggs	# of Nestlings	Known Fledglings	Possible Fledglings	Occup. Status
RTHA	Lower Condor Gulch	*HIPPO-2	<2/4										Occupied
RTHA	McCabe Canyon	MC-3		<4/8	4/13-15	5/29-30				2	2	2	2
RTHA	North Balconies	NB-7	<1/31	<4/3	4/6-8	5/25-27				4	2	4	4
RTHA	North Wilderness Trail	NWT-1	<1/17	<4/7	4/7-9	5/26-28				2	1	2	2
RTHA	South Wilderness North	SWN-2	<1/4	<3/15	4/11-13	5/25-26				4	4	4	4
RTHA	South Wilderness Rock	SWR-2	<2/15	<4/14	4/17-19	5/20-23				2	0	2	2
RTHA	Upper Condor Gulch	HIPPO-2	<2/4	<4/23				<5/16			0	0	Failed
RSHA	Bench Area	BA-3	<2/25	<4/7	4/13-15	5/31-6/2				2	2	2	2
RSHA	Kingman Land South	*PCG-6	<2/27										Occupied
RSHA	McCabe Canyon	MC-5			4/12-15	5/27-30				2	2	2	2
RSHA	Pinnacles Campground	PCG-5	<2/27	<4/18				<5/18		0	0	0	Failed
RSHA	Pinnacles Campground	PCG-6	<2/27		4/4-5	5/19-20				3	3	3	3
RSHA	Regan Ranch Canyon	RR-4		<4/19				<6/5		0	0	0	Failed
RSHA	South Wilderness Trail		<3/15										Occupied

Note: for the "Occup. Status" column, # refers to possible fledglings, "Occupied" = territorial occupation, "Not Occ." = no occupation, "Failed" = failed nest, "Unknown" = breeding confirmed (see nest code) or likely, but nest status unknown. For the "Nest Code" column, * refers to territorial links for raptor pairs occupying more than 1 territory.

Appendix C. 2011 nest phenology and success for accipiters, kites, and owls (barn owls, long-eared owls, great-horned owls, and Western screech-owls).

Nest Species	Territory Occupied	Nest Code	Arrival Date	Begin Incub	Hatch Date	Fledge Date	Abandon Date	Failed Date	# of Eggs	# of Nestlings	Known Fledglings	Possible Fledglings	Occup. Status
COHA	Kingman Land North	KLN-15		<4/19	5/17-20	6/19-21				2	2	2	2
COHA	Kingman Land South		<6/5										Occupied
COHA	Marion Canyon	MAR-4		<4/13	5/25-28	6/25-27				2	2	2	2
COHA	South Wilderness Trail	SWT-7	<3/15	<4/14				<6/22		0	0	0	Failed
SSHA	Peaks View Area	PVA-4		<5/13	6/9-13	7/5-6				4	4	4	4
WTKI	Double Gates												Not Occ.
WTKI	Jawbone Canyon	JAW-1		<4/21	5/12-15	6/15-16				1	1	1	1
WTKI	Kingman Land North												Not Occ.
WTKI	Kingman Land South	KLS-9	<4/8	<5/4	5/22-31	6/25-27				3	3	3	3
WTKI	Marion Canyon												Not Occ.
WTKI	McCabe Canyon		<5/3										Occupied
WTKI	S Wilderness – N End		<4/14										Occupied
BNOW	D. Soto Canyon	DS-3	<1/7	<2/22									Unknown
BNOW	Grassy Canyon		<2/23										Occupied
BNOW	Kingman Land South		<3/2										Occupied
LEOW	Grassy Canyon												Occupied
LEOW	Kingman Land North	KLN-7		<4/1	4/1-5	4/20-23				4	4	4	4
LEOW	Marion Canyon												Not Occ.
LEOW	McCabe Canyon		<5/3										Occupied
GHOW	Chalone Picnic Area	*WCP-2	<1/11										Occupied
GHOW	Guard Rock		<5/5										Occupied
GHOW	High Pks W of CPA	WCP-2	<1/1		3/27-4/2	5/29-6/7				2	0		2
GHOW	Kingman Land North		<2/15										Occupied
GHOW	McCabe Canyon	MC-4	<2/15		2/25-27	5/1-3				2	2	2	2
GHOW	North Wilderness Rock	NWR-3			3/14-17	5/19-23				2	2	2	2
WESO	Chalone Housing Area		<2/9										Occupied
WESO	Upper Bear Gulch		<1/29										Occupied
WESO	Headquarters		<1/15										Occupied

Note: for the **"Occup. Status"** column, # refers to possible fledglings, "Occupied" = territorial occupation, "Not Occ." = no occupation, "Failed" = failed nest, "Unknown" = breeding confirmed (see nest code) or likely, but nest status unknown. For the **"Nest Code"** column, * refers to territorial links for raptor pairs occupying more than 1 territory.

Appendix D. Documentation of changes in data collection methods.

No changes were made to data collection methods for the Pinnacles raptor monitoring program through the course of the 2011 season. In 2010, several changes were made to procedures for entering observations into raptor monitoring databases, and relevant sections in the Raptor Monitoring Protocol were revised accordingly. Primarily these changes were put in place to address Inventory & Monitoring standards for data management and storage, and the development of a more efficient workflow and structuring of existing MS Access databases. These changes were detailed in the 2010 annual report and are briefly reviewed below.

Through the 2010 season raptor observations and breeding summaries were entered into the "Breeding Raptors" Access database, after development was finalized in 2007-2008. To increase efficient statistical analysis of prairie falcon occupancy and productivity, additional fields were created in the database "Data Entry" form, including fields detailing detection purpose, survey intention, confirmation of territorial behavior, and prairie falcon detection. The SFAN I&M data manager is currently completing raptor database revisions to include end-of-season breeding summary queries for number of territories occupied, territorial pairs, nesting pairs, successful nests, total nestlings, nestlings per nest, possible fledglings, and fledglings per nest. The revised raptor database will be used for data collection and management in upcoming seasons.

The 2011 Prairie Falcon Monitoring Protocol was peer reviewed via a blind review process through the task agreement with the University of Washington (UW). Dr. James Agee of UW and Dr. Penelope Latham , PWR I&M program manager, coordinated and evaluated responses to all peer review comments, successfully completing a 5-year process of protocol design and revisions.

Appendix E. Public interest highlights.

The 2011 breeding season was the 26th year of raptor monitoring at Pinnacles. Field observations began 1 January 2011 and ended 13 July 2011, with a total of over 150 possible and active nest sites monitored during 808 observation hours. Climbing advisories were put into effect in January to reduce nest disturbance by visitors, updated to reflect unoccupied territories in March, and lifted in July at the end of the raptor breeding season.

- The NPS Raptor Biologist conducted prairie falcon nest entries at 2 Pinnacles prairie falcon eyries with raptor researcher Dr. Doug Bell from East Bay Regional Park District, during the 2011 season. All falcon nestlings at the North Chalone Peak and South Balconies nests were briefly handled, banded, and blood samples were obtained. All nestlings at these 2 eyries fledged successfully. Banding and blood sample information collected in 2009-2011 will be used to ascertain genetic insularity and pair fidelity in the Pinnacles prairie falcon population.

- Eleven breeding raptor species and 44 nests were confirmed in the monument.

- Seven sensitive species were confirmed breeding this year: prairie falcon, peregrine falcon, golden eagle, Cooper's hawk, sharp-shinned hawk, white-tailed kite, and long-eared owl.

- For the 7th consecutive year a peregrine falcon pair was documented nesting at the monument. The site produced 3 nestlings but failed to fledge any young. The last previously confirmed peregrine falcon nest effort at Pinnacles was documented in 1957.

- Accipiter species were confirmed nesting in the monument, with the 10th sharp-shinned hawk nest ever documented.

- Twenty breeding records for raptor species at Pinnacles were reported to the Santa Cruz Predatory Bird Research Group and the California Natural Diversity Database (through the California Department of Fish and Game).

- An ArcMap project was updated to visually display GPS and GIS information relating to the raptor monitoring program, including historical nest sites, monitoring watch spots, nest distribution by geologic and habitat layers, and locations of advisory signs posted at Pinnacles.

- All raptor advisory signs were affixed to metal brackets in cement foundations to make the signs more secure and to prevent their theft and movement.

- The 4th annual Rockpile Rendezvous – a centennial event to emphasize climber contributions, history, and management at Pinnacles over the past 60 years – was organized by the raptor biologist, drawing in the local climbing community and providing visitors with information on historical resource and recreation management at the monument

NPS 114/116504, August 2012